Boston

on old pic

1. An Edwardian postcard of Bargate published by E.W. Peakome, who produced wonderfully animated cards of the Boston area, with the "Red Lion" pub on the right and The Stump towering over the scene.

£3.95

Introduction

Boston is a large and ancient market town and port on the River Witham with a population of 35,000. It derives its name from St Botolph, the patron saint of the parish church, generally known as Boston Stump. It is a Gothic structure with a 282-foot high tower. Like most large churches, it was built and added to over several centuries. The foundations were laid in the early years of the 14th century but it was completed some 200 years later.

The docks also have a very long history and as early as the 13th century Boston was a staple port for wool, leather, tin and lead. Today it mainly handles steel, timber and grain. The town has many interesting buildings besides The Stump, including the Guildhall, Hussey's Tower and Shodfriars, but I have not included cards of these buildings because a three-line caption would not do them justice and in any case the postcards are quite easy to find.

The town is also associated with the Pilgrim Fathers. Some 400 years ago, a number of nonconformists attempted to emigrate to Holland but they were caught and imprisoned for a short time, probably in the Guildhall. They were successful in their mission a few years later but this time via the Humber. Some of their number returned to England and with others set sail for America in *The Mayflower*.

There is plenty to see in Boston, and on Wednesdays it holds probably the most traditional market you would find anywhere.

For the non-Bostonian there may be some confusion with the River Witham and The Haven. Boston stands astride the River Witham but the section from the Sluice Bridge onwards through the town is known as The Haven!

In Boston today you will hear people speaking several European languages. This is because it is greatly involved in the agricultural, horticultural and food processing industries and as these are labour-intensive industries, it has attracted immigrants from all over Europe and beyond and many have settled in the town.

Most of the postcards in this book date from pre-1914. Boston in the Edwardian era (1901-10) had a population of just over 20,000

Eric Croft
July 2011

Picture postcards were first published in Britain in 1894, but it was not until a decade later that they began to take off, when in 1902 the Post Office allowed a message to be written on the address side. This meant that the whole of one side was available for the picture and obviously gave more scope to publishers. Photographic viewcards became very popular, and the postcard developed into the most important way of communicating news or messages, in much the same way as the telephone is used today. The years up to 1914 were the 'Golden Age' of picture postcards, when millions of imaginative designs covering every subject under the sun were published by a host of national, regional and local firms or individuals. These latter published postcards of streets, buildings and events locally, and have left us with an amazing pictorial record of the early 20th century. Boston had the excellent E.W. Peakome, who published superb photographic postcards of local views and events, F. & G. Beale, E. Gray, Hackfords, and a publisher with the initials 'ER', probably E. Rowett. The town was also covered by Jackson of Grimsby and national firms Valentine of Dundee, Photochrom, Boots and W.H. Smith. Where known, the publisher of the card is included in the caption.

2. The Stump dominates the town from all angles. This postcard was published by Jackson & Son of Grimsby in their 'Jay-em-Jay' series.

3. The Stump from the riverside on a card published by the Photochrom Co. of Tunbridge Wells.

4. Boston Market Place with the "Angel Hotel" in the centre and a fairground roundabout set up on the right. Another Peakome card.

5. A postcard showing the Market Place. Posted to Market Deeping in January 1905, the message reads *" I hope you will like this. The mark on the other side is over our shop. You will see Clark a little to left. That is a tobacco shop".* This card was published by 'E.R.', possibly E. Rowett.

6. An anonymously-published card of the Market Place c.1905. The shop on the right advertises 'cheapest in England for window glass'.

7. J.H. Small's wholesale draper's shop is on the left at no. 15, with Chamberlain's Hotel on the left and Hurst's Pharmacy right. This card was published by the newsagents W.H. Smith, which produced its own postcards nationwide.

8. A marvellous aerial view of the Market Place and the May Fair, taken by E.W. Peakome from the tower of St. Botolph's Church. The statue in the foreground is the Herbert Ingrams Memorial. The card was posted to Sheffield in July 1905.

CHAMBERLAIN'S
COMMERCIAL HOUSE
DRAPERS
J.H.SMALL & SON
MILLINERS
J.H.SMALL & SON
COSTUMIERS
HURST'S
PHARMACY.
HURST
DINING ROOMS
FREEMAN
HARDY & WILLIS
BOSTON.

9. The Docks on another card by E.W. Peakome. This shows the extent of the timber trade at the docks and it is equally important today, over 100 years after this photograph was taken.

10. Another busy docks scene. The ship in the centre looks like a naval vessel, probably on a 'visit' which may explain why there are so many people on the dockside. The card was sent to White & Co., offal merchants of Boston in September 1906 with the intriguing message: *" Hope to see you in the market today. Am going to have a bit of fishing this morning. Book me 5 tons of sharps. Isn't he a swanker, anyone would think he kept pigs!"*

11. A 'Kingsway' series postcard from W.H. Smith of the docks, posted to Aisthorpe, Lincoln, in 1906. In the centre is a dredger owned by a London company. In view of the distance the docks are from the open sea, I imagine dredgers were a common sight.

12. A postcard published by Valentine of Dundee featuring the not very originally named paddle steamer *Boston* and posted to Stickney in July 1905. I assume the message *" Dada has gone for a tidal trip tonight"* means a trip on this steamer which took passengers on tours into The Wash.

13. Much use was made of the river in Boston, both for commercial and leisure purposes. Here we have a card of a Regatta near the Sluice Bridge (where the river is not tidal) by local photographer 'ER'. It was posted at Boston in November 1904.

14. A fishing match in progress on the river at Cow Bridge on a card published in the G.B. & Sons series and posted at Sheffield in June 1904.

15. Leisure activities on the River Witham included rowing, by the look of the number of boats for hire! This is another W.H. Smith-published card, posted from Leicester in October 1918.

16. A good view of the Grand Sluice Bridge published by 'ER', with more rowing boats for hire.

17. A fine photographic view of the River Witham on a card by an unidentified publisher.

18. The Doughty Quay on Boston's High Street pictured on a c.1910 postcard published by Photochrom. The large building in the centre of the picture is known as Van Smirren's Warehouse, though this firm, which manufactured fish paste and other products, vacated the premises some years ago.

19. The swing bridge over the River Witham on a photographic card from F. & G. Beale of Boston. This bridge marks the end of the tidal river for boats travelling inland.

20. Though this postcard was published c.1905, it actually shows an ox-roast at celebrations marking the Golden Jubilee of Queen Victoria in 1887.

21. A deserted Bargate on a card posted to Easingwold in July 1906 and published by F. & G. Beale.

22. The old Town Bridge on a card posted on 2 May 1914 bearing the message: *" This photo was taken the last day the Old Bridge was up - you can see Ernest on the ladder"*. Ernest has one foot on the ladder and the other on a ledge on the Corn Exchange, some 20 feet from the ground! This was obviously pre-health and safety days!

23. The New Town Bridge, incorporating street lamps on the pavement, on a card posted from Boston to Wainfleet in January 1914. As on the previous card, Boots Cash Chemists are on the right and Loveley's Commercial Hotel in the centre distance. Both photographers have used a horse and cart to enliven the scene, while this one also features a motor car. Card published by W.H. Smith.

24. The Post Office decorated for the 1911 coronation on a card published by Boston photographer E. Gray. It looks as though the whole staff turned out for the photograph but, strangely, there is not a woman to be seen!

25. The statue of Herbert Ingram situated in the Market Square. Mr Ingram was the founder of the *Illustrated London News*, a local businessman and MP for the town in the 1850s. The effigy of the woman pouring water at the base of the statue symbolises the clean water supply in the town which came about partly due to Mr Ingram's influence. Card sent to Hull in July 1907. *" Rained hard this morning. Did not get a photo"*, wrote Fred.

26. A card by the local firm of Hackfords of Church Close, Boston, showing a river pageant celebrating the coronation of King George V in 1911.

27. Another card by Hackfords, unused and undated but probably another view of the 1911 coronation pageant.

28. The bakers' football team on an unused and undated postcard from local photographer E. Gray. Most towns at this time had football teams from the local shops, including bakers, butchers, tailors etc., and they usually played the matches on half-day closing afternoons.

29. A wonderful view of Boston's steam engine in action on 26 June 1908 at a large fir

th Square. This is another card by local photographers Hackfords.

30. Another view of the same fire and by the same photographer.

31. St. Botolph's undergoing restoration in 1932. *"I am just looking at the church as I write. This scaffolding partly down now. A carnival here all week for hospital, such processions I never saw before. Been grand weather till 3 p.m. then rain"*. The card was posted to a Sheffield address.

32. The very aptly-named Tower Street on another 'ER' card which was posted in June 1906, strangely in Stockton on Tees and addressed to Putney!

33. Main Ridge, again on an 'ER' card, this one posted in September 1904. It bears the cryptic message: *" I beg to remind you that there is such a street as the one in the photo"*.

34. Rowel Row on yet another 'ER' card. It has not been posted but is from the same 1904/5 period as the others and again the kids have turned out, including twins in the pram on the left!

35. Carlton Road, this time on a card published by E. Gray and again posted in 1904 - to Newark-on-Trent.

36. A wonderfully animated card of West Street by Jackson of Grimsby in their 'Jay-em-Jay' series. It is not dated but the vehicles would suggest it is from the 1910-12 period. On the left is the shop of the wonderfully diverse C.W. Gale - antiseptic, hairdresser, tobacconist, fishing tackle!

37. An undated but probably 1920s view of Strait Bargate by Wing & Co., whose sign can be seen on a building almost in the centre of the card.

38. Another street scene by 'ER'. This is Liquorpond Street and dates from 1904. I think 'ER' must have photographed every street in Boston and he usually managed to gather a crowd - a good idea if their parents each bought a few cards. On the right of the street is a sign for 'The Little Wonder'.

THE LITTLE
WONDER
E·R 107·

39. The children of Broadfield Street obviously saw 'ER' setting up his camera! The card was posted from Boston to Nottingham in December 1904.

40. Posted in Boston in May 1908, this anonymously-published card shows Mr Dion's butchers cart. His shop was in Pen Street. The location of this scene is uncertain, but it looks to be outside a pub.

41. The premises of Geo. L. Wilson, family grocer, provision merchant and tea specialist, at the corner of Wormgate and Red Lion Street. He sent this postcard (which carries his details on the back) to a farmer at Wyberton West on 8 September 1909, asking him not to send the ducks that week but a week on Saturday!

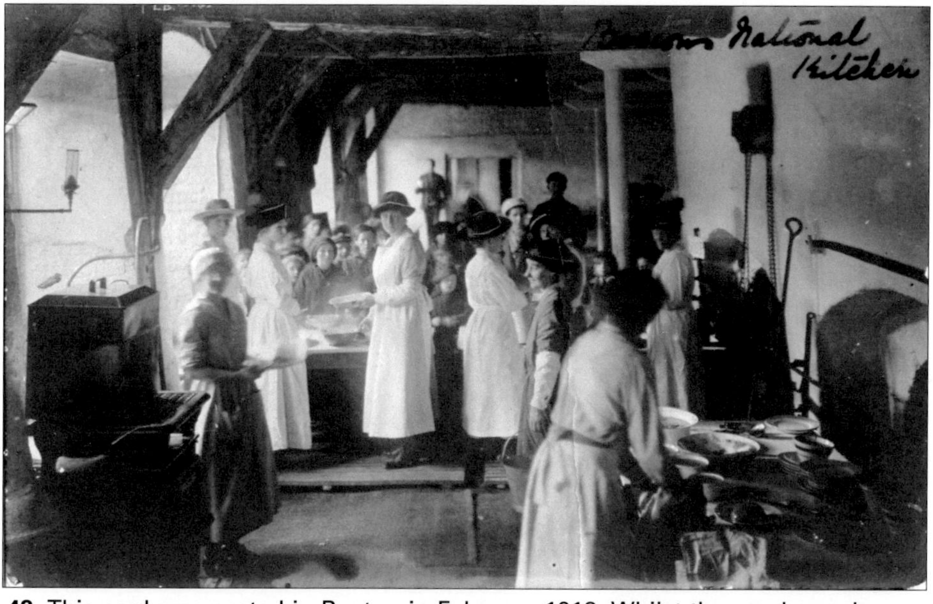

42. This card was posted in Boston in February 1918. Whilst the sender makes no mention of the picture in the message, fortunately he wrote 'Boston's National Kitchen' on the front. I assume this refers to the National Kitchens set up by Lord Rhondda to encourage people to 'eat out', thereby saving on fuel. A nice piece of social history.

43. This superb postcard shows Simpson & Sons delivery outfit outside these shops in the Market Place. It would appear they had only recently acquired the engine because the previous owner's name 'G H Kent, Maud Street Saw Mills' can be seen on the name-board on the engine, but it has been crudely painted over.

44. A view of the unveiling ceremony at the impressive War Memorial on 25 September 1921.

45. A rather deserted view of Boston station on a typical W.H. Smith card. I think the firm of national newsagents published a card of every station in the country where they had a book stall. This card was posted on 10 December 1915 to Mary Plant in Rochdale. The sender was hoping to see his sweetheart in a fortnight and he was " *counting the hours*"!

46. The Holland County Council Offices on a trade card produced by the Bath & Portland Stone Firms Ltd in 1926.

47. A view of the crowd (all wearing hats!) at the Lincolnshire Show, which was held in Boston in 1912, on land on Spilsby Road. The card was published by Boston photographer E. Gray.

48. A well-attended football match when Boston played Gainsborough on 20 April 1922. This looks like a certain goal but nobody is looking at the ball! An anonymously-published card - I wonder if he sold many at 3d. each!

49. Maud Foster Mill takes its name from the drain it stands alongside. It is also known as Ostler's Mill after the name of the miller. It was fully restored a few years ago and is well worth a visit. This card was published by E. Peakome and was posted to Walthamstow in 1904.

50. The same mill, this time actually captioned Ostler's Mill. The card was published in the 'Empire View Series', Doncaster, and probably dates from the 1930s.

51. A view of The Cannons by 'ER' which stood on Wide Bargate on a card posted to Crowborough, Sussex, in April 1905. The cannon were presented to the town at the end of the Crimean War. They then did their bit in the Second World War when they were scrapped as part of the war effort!

52. Another 'lost landmark'. The stocks, like the cannon, also stood in Wide Bargate with the cattle pens in the background. They look to be almost new on this card posted at Manchester in July 1907, so they were obviously replacements. However, they fell into disrepair and were removed in the 1950s.

53. This fire occurred sometime in 1905 and was photographed for this postcard by E. Gray of Boston. It was at the premises of Cooke & Co., 27 Strait Bargate, which is the site now occupied by W.H. Smith.

54. This view by Hackford is at the junction of High Street and the Town Bridge. It is unused and undated but I think it could be a view of the official opening ceremony of the New Town Bridge which was constructed in 1913. C.J. Wilson's shop is in the centre of the card and it bears the words 'Civet Cat' each side of his name.

55. This is the original Wesleyan Chapel on a card posted to Mr. Rylatt at The Gas Works, Port Elizabeth, South Africa. *" I expect the 1st Sleaford staff to be at this place on Thursday"*, wrote the sender. I wonder who they were?

56. The Wesleyan Chapel on fire on 29 June 1909. The postcard was sent by Edith to her mother at Hackthorn, Lincoln, in October that year, but as is often the case, she doesn't say a word about the event, instead concentrating on family affairs: *"Sorry to say Auntie does not get on very fast. Uncle has got a very bad cold and has gone to Grimsby today. Auntie's cold is much better. I am enjoying myself very much. I went to the big tea last Monday"*.

57. Another view of the Chapel fire. I originally thought the onlookers were very close to the fire with a lad stood almost on the chapel steps! On closer examination, however, the card was obvious as a fake, and the flames have been added by scratches to the negative!

58. The new Wesleyan Chapel, rebuilt to a new design after the 1909 fire. This is another card from Edith to her mother, posted in August 1911. Again there is no mention of the view; she just says the weather is very hot and that she is reading 'East Lynne'!

59. Another pageant or procession but not used or dated. The sign at the top right reads 'Mather & Co. Garage', which was at the "White Hart Hotel".